Understanding Cryptocurrency

Anonymity in Blockchain & Altcoins

By Scott S. Bergman

ISBN-13: 978-1984117335
ISBN-10: 1984117335

TABLE OF CONTENTS

CHAPTER 4. WHY ANONYMITY IS SUCH A BIG DEAL TO SOME USERS........................19

CHAPTER 5. SOME ANONYMITY PROPOSALS IN CRYPTO 24

Introduction

About the eBook

Over the past few months, interest in cryptocurrency trading has increased and, as a result, blockchain technology.

The definition of blockchain technology is that it is a digital ledger that is not corruptible and records digital transactions. It works on a network with several nodes (individual participants).

Once a party makes a transaction, it goes through a verification process to achieve a consensus. After there is a consensus, the transaction is valid. No one party can edit any of the entries alone, hence the incorruptibility.

Blockchain technology is here to make sure that we get rid of third parties in our transactions. Not only can we have a cheaper transaction, but we are also able to transfer large amounts of cash in a single transaction.

The reasons for reading the book

If you are searching for a comprehensive, but straightforward, guide on the intricacies of blockchain technology and, more specifically, the subject of anonymity, this book is for you.

Not only will you get all the intricate facts in simple English, but you will also make more informed decisions with regards to cryptocurrencies.

What the reader will gain in the end

After completing this read, you will:
- Have an understanding of blockchain technology
- Know how anonymity works
- Know which cryptocurrencies indeed have anonymity
- Understand why governments have a problem with the anonymity concept
- Be able to assess the investment attractiveness of some altcoins
- Find out which of the altcoins should be considered when creating an investment portfolio.

Chapter 1. A recap of how cryptocurrencies work

Before we go any further, we should first try to understand a few basic terminologies that relate to how cryptocurrencies work.

The Distributed Ledger

You have most likely heard about a ledger in your day-to-day activities. It might have been your bookkeeper or accountant, or even from your bank.
Earlier civilizations kept traditional ledgers on paper. As time passed and technology advanced, it became digital, but could still suffer malicious manipulation since the saved data was in one location.

The distributed ledger is more of a duplicated ledger hosted on several computers in a network. There is no one holding area, which limits susceptibility to digital attacks. Once there is an entry, all the nodes in the network receive the information, and a majority has to agree to it for the transaction to be valid.

The distribution makes the transaction safer because there is no central point of data entry and editing. Also, if one party's transaction is compromised, all the participants in the network would need to be compromised, which is highly improbable.

The Consensus Algorithm

Cryptocurrencies run on distributed systems. The one problem in the system is that of consensus, which entails finding and getting to the point of stability in light of several unstable conditions.

The consensus problem's solution comes about when we achieve stability in a distributed system.

Peer-to-Peer transactions

The main feature of a peer-to-peer transaction is the elimination of middlemen or a central system. Cryptocurrency transactions take place between two parties (peers) in a network.

The transactions are more transparent and cost less than those that include intermediaries. Further, since the peer-to-peer transactions are on a distributed ledger, they give a sense of security to the parties in the transaction.

The Types of Community Members

The types of community members vary from one coin to another, but also depends on the network powering the coin. For instance, the blockchain community consists of miners, who participate in the mining of coins as well as the verification of transactions. We also have the clients, or the people who transact using the mined currency.

If the network does not depend on verification, there is an additional participant called the master node, or the leader that tells the other nodes what to do.

The blockchain technology which powers Bitcoin runs on the premise of 51% consensus. At least more than half of the network members have to agree with the transaction for it to pass.

Other coins, such as PIVX, Zcash and Dash, use another method, where one of the network members acts as a master node. The master node leads the other members of the network. One individual operates the master node; there is also a server that is decentralized.

The master node also has to have a bond with a cryptocurrency. The master node is rewarded mostly by transaction costs.

The main advantage of being a master node is that you may end up passively earning a nice sum.

The main disadvantage is that you may lose your investment if the coin does not do well.

Recap: Cryptocurrencies have come at the most opportune time. The evolution of cryptocurrency will change how transactions take place from now on.

The blockchain network is also a welcome invention. For a very long time, centralized transactions have been the norm. The technology has even opened up peer-to-peer transactions, which have become very popular in recent times. We have taken the liberty to learn about how they work.

Chapter 2. The anonymity concept in Cryptocurrency

First of all, to accurately define cryptocurrency, we need to differentiate it from privacy.

So, what is privacy in cryptocurrency?

Privacy comes into play when you perform a transaction and do not store any of the particulars of the transactions anywhere. For instance, if you purchase 20 units of a cryptocurrency, for say $400 a piece, and the type of currency, the number of units and amount paid is not logged, that is privacy.

Anonymity, on the other hand, is a situation where the identity of the person performing transactions is hidden.

Some cryptocurrencies are anonymous, but not that many.

The Origin of Cryptocurrency

Bitcoin is by far the most common cryptocurrency there is to date. The inventor, Satoshi Nakamoto, came up with the currency in 2009. The decision to look for a better method of transacting was a result of the 2008 economic crisis.

When the economy started misbehaving, the central banks just minted more money to ensure a 1930s catastrophe would not repeat itself. The increase in the supply of cash automatically decreased its value, and this power, for Satoshi, was just too much for one body to have.

He had a dream of a monetary system existing that would be decentralized, which meant no one person could control it. The forces of demand and supply would be the only ones at play, and this would make economies more stable.

The Blockchain technology that runs Bitcoin is on a distributed network. In a distributed system, there is no one central point of storage of data, making it difficult to launch attacks.

The success of Bitcoin prompted the creation of other cryptocurrencies. Some of these coins came about as a result of Bitcoin hard forks, whereas others emerged as a result of independent innovations. For example, Zerocoin is a product of a Bitcoin hard fork.

Some of the other coins that have no connection with Bitcoin also have forks that give birth to new coins. The Dash coin's fork, for instance, gave birth to PIVX. The resulting altcoin is usually an improvement of the 'mother coin.'

Anonymity as a natural choice in peer-to-peer technology

Moving to peer-to-peer technology is a revolution that has been a long time coming. As with everything else, the client always wants more. Most people move from the centralized system to the decentralized one to avoid scrutiny.

Anonymity and avoiding surveillance go hand-in-hand. If your transactions are sensitive, the peer-to-peer technology would be an optimal choice since it eliminates third parties. The less prying eyes there are, the better the protection of your data.

It is also challenging to attack what you do not know. Anonymity helps people stay away from cyber attacks and theft of money.

The Good, The Bad and the Ugly in Anonymity

Let us start with the good. When you open a bank account, you will have to give personal details, such as your ID number, driver's license or passport. This information can be used to track you; all your transactions are logged in the bank's server.

If, for instance, somebody is looking for your account, all they need to do is hack your banker, and they will find a treasure trove of information there. Someone may transfer all your money, and it may be complicated to recover it.

If your transaction details could be anonymous, such losses would be easy to avoid, which is why anonymity is very attractive.

When we get to the bad, some people want anonymity for all the wrong reasons. The reason why several governments are freaking out about cryptocurrencies is because it may render fiat currency archaic. While for the citizens the revolution of the coin may be a good thing, the states will no longer be in control of what citizens do with their money.

It is even scarier to imagine that many governments may no longer have the ability to collect revenue for development purposes. Money laundering and tax evasion are some of the bad results of having cryptocurrencies as dominant currencies.

When we delve deeper, cryptocurrency anonymity may just help the perpetuation of some very grievous crimes. Later in this book, we will cover a few anonymous software that have links with the darknet.

The darknet is the internet's black market and may as well be the online version of the underworld. We all know what happens in the underworld. There are no rules in the dark. If you want anything, all you need is money, and you can find it.

Now, picture a situation where we have an untraceable network and untraceable currencies. There will be buying and selling of drugs and weapons, and security forces will be flying blind.

The blockchain network can be used for currency transfer as well as other digital properties.

Recap: At this point, we cannot deny that anonymity in transactions is here for good. The harder the government tries to fight this, the worse it will get. There should probably be a way to regulate the coins, but that may be a challenge.

Currently, the internet can give birth to anything. Unless we get rid of the internet altogether, cryptocurrencies will continue to grow.

We also cannot dispute the fact that there can be problems that arise with abusing anonymity.

Chapter 3. Why Bitcoin Struggles with the anonymity question

It is not a secret that governments do not like Bitcoin. The states view cryptocurrency as a way for wayward citizens circumnavigate the law.

Cryptocurrencies also make most country governments jittery by threatening their monopolistic control of their respective economies. The states also just want to ensure the markets work within the confines of demand and supply without compromise.

The Chinese government, for instance, shut down Initial Coin offerings (ICOs) and is looking to close down cryptocurrency exchanges soon. The reason for such drastic steps from China is mainly political. Its political structure is not conducive to competing for currency and the banking system going rogue. Only time will tell if outlawing cryptos will work for China or not.

The US government is not far behind in efforts to stop Bitcoin from being anonymous. In 2016, the

Internal Revenue Service (IRS) filed a petition in a California court. The summons required Coinbase, a cryptocurrency exchange, to furnish the IRS with data regarding its users from 2013 to 2015.

The UK, in the same breath, is seeking to bring cryptocurrency exchanges within anti-drug and anti-money laundering laws. The most significant fear the UK government has concerning Bitcoin is its anonymity, which is allegedly a fertile breeding ground for tax evasion, money laundering and acts of terrorism.

Let us just be fair and say that the governments have a good reason to be concerned. The only question left will be whether the steps taken will tame Bitcoin.

The reason for attaching the 'anonymous' tag to Bitcoin

For the longest time, Bitcoin has been thought of as an anonymous cryptocurrency, especially for beginners.

The truth is that anonymity is very limited. Blockchain, which is the technology that runs Bitcoin, cannot allow that. The first step to trading on a Bitcoin exchange is to create a wallet. The processes are comprehensive. Most wallets use two-factor authentication, which makes use of other accounts, such as your emails.

Some of the reasons why some may think Bitcoin is anonymous include:

- The transactions are not directly tied to the identities of the individuals transacting.
- Bitcoin addresses are random, and any person can create an address without necessarily giving their details.
- Data transmitting and forwarding happens between several random nodes in the blockchain network.

How Bitcoin's anonymity is defeated

While we would like to believe Bitcoin is anonymous, it can only be pseudo-anonymous. The blockchain workings defeat the anonymity claim.

When transactions take place on the blockchain, there is deanonymization for clustering to happen. The clustering can open you up to unmasking. All your transactions will be clustered together, and if someone can get to one node, they can uncover your identity.

If someone has enough power, they can launch a brute force attack on you. They need to focus a massive amount of power in your wallet and retrieve your private keys. Remember, once you lose your private keys, you also lose the cryptocurrency associated with them.

If you use the same Gmail account as you use in your Bitcoin wallet, you may also be vulnerable. Also, try to avoid using two-factor authentification that relies on text messages. Cryptographic security keys are more secure than SMS.

The problem of transaction clustering

Clustering in data mining is grouping all transactions that are similar in the same cluster. This grouping is detrimental to the anonymity claim in Bitcoin for two reasons.

First of all, when clustering takes place, there is deanonymization. This means that the origins of transactions are traceable.

Secondly, the clustering process involves the grouping of transactions that are similar or are made by one person. This ultimately defeats the purpose of randomization because someone observing the clustering process can easily piece the information together and uncover the real-life identity of the person performing the transactions.

How to improve Bitcoin's anonymity

With the passage of time, more Bitcoin users want to have anonymity in their transactions. For some time now, there have been efforts to make Bitcoin more anonymous.

Zerocoin is a bitcoin extension that is considered the solution to Bitcoin's anonymity woes. Zerocoin eliminates the dependence on third parties to validate ownership of a digital coin.

Here, you can mint coins by burning them up. Later, you can take back your currency by getting a new coin with no history of transactions. The new coin cannot be traced back to any previous transactions, and this dramatically increases the anonymity of trading.

Recap: Bitcoin has had a long, hard fight with its claims of anonymity for a long time. There is a lot of effort towards ensuring it becomes completely anonymous; it may take some time.

It is the hope of many that zero coins will finally put an end the search for a completely anonymous coin. Time will tell whether or not it will be foolproof.

Chapter 4. Why anonymity is such a big deal to some users

Cryptocurrencies have become very popular over the last few years because of their anonymity claim.

Some individuals and businesses find the anonymous tag given to cryptocurrencies very attractive for a few reasons:
- Security of funds.
- Hiding in plain sight. This is better explained with an analogy. Assuming you have plans to do something big with your business, if you transfer a large amount of cash for the event,

the information may leak because banks are full of employees, and people love to talk. As such, the information is likely to reach your competitors. In short, anonymity helps you hide your plans until you are ready to reveal them.

- Safeguarding of sensitive transactions among others.

The libertarian nature of the cryptocurrency promise

There has always been some centralization of fiat money since the beginning of civilization. In the present day, countries' central banks have always controlled the way money flows. Not everybody is happy with how much control these institutions have over the economies they govern.

This may surprise many, but a loaf of bread famously cost a whopping billion worth of worthless Zimbabwean dollars just a few years ago.

It happened after the authoritarian government ran the resident currency to the ground with the uncontrolled printing of money. In fact, Bitcoin is currently very popular there because of its incorruptible finite nature.

Many people, for instance, do not agree that governments should have the power to devalue currencies and many other such actions.

The battle of decentralization versus the status quo

We cannot stress enough the fears that plague the governments with regards to cryptocurrencies and their anonymity. There have been several efforts to make sure that cryptocurrency clients come out of the woodwork.

Over the last few years, there has been a bit of a gold rush in the trading of cryptos. We all know what happens when there is no longer a demand for a commodity with a high supply. If demand dwindles, the price drops, and it may become extinct.

One of the best ways that governments can maintain control over their citizenry is by controlling the economy. Governments are concerned because if the demand for digital cash surpasses that of fiat currency, they will lose their grip.

Therefore, some countries are banning cryptocurrencies; some are calling for cryptocurrency exchanges to divulge information about their clients.

Cybercrime, Drugs, Money Laundering and Tax Evasion fears

The most significant factor that sends chills down the spines of the powers that be is that cryptocurrencies will help perpetuate crimes.

These fears are valid. There have been several cases in which companies have been held ransom by cybercriminals, and all they wanted was cryptocurrency payments.

The anonymity concept is what made the committers of these crimes very bold; they knew they could get away with these actions without any repercussions.

It also seems like a perfect vehicle for other crimes, such as money laundering and drugs. Since the transactions are deemed anonymous and large purchases do not raise any eyebrows, anything can happen. Dirty money is easily used to buy cryptocurrencies and then 'washed' and made clean, and nobody is any the wiser.

The fear of rampant tax evasion is also valid. Businesses would no longer need to have all their transactions go through their banks and undergo scrutiny. Once you find a few rogue, well-paying clients, you merely get them to agree to buy goods and services using cryptocurrencies, and the IRS would not be aware. These few clients duplicated over several businesses could be a big problem since the federal government would lose a lot of revenue.

The balance between privacy and security

As we mentioned earlier, there is a thin line between privacy and anonymity, despite the fact that some people may use them interchangeably.

Privacy protects the details of a transaction, whereas anonymity safeguards the identity of individuals involved in a trade.

Many cryptocurrencies have some level of anonymity, but those run over blockchain have very little to no privacy. Private transactions are a bit of a fallacy because at least 51% of the nodes in the network have to agree on their validity.

Recap: While the demand for anonymity is rising exponentially, there is also a need to look at the specific reasons behind the requirement.

While some individuals just want to stay in the shadows, there is a group of people out to use the anonymity that cryptocurrency trading provides for evil.

Governments are worried that this kind of veil can hide criminals who will end up bringing economies to their knees. They have cause to worry and will continue to try and make cryptocurrencies less and less anonymous.

The fight against cryptocurrencies is going to be a very long and hard fight since the currencies are also pushing back by trying to improve their anonymity scale daily.

Chapter 5. Some anonymity proposals in crypto

I2P

I2P, or the Invisible Internet Project is an anonymizing software. The software protects the hosts of various websites that we may not find on the conventional search engines we use, such as Google, Bing, and others.

It works as a network within a network. I2P protects you from surveillance by ISPs that may want to keep an eye on you.

They offer services that include plugins for serverless emails, anonymous web browsing, anonymous web hosting, among others. Your communications on I2P are not traceable.

However, this software has had links to various criminal activities. I2P is supposedly home to the darknet giant Silk Road. Silk Road is known as the most significant online black market where you can get anything, including drugs.

TOR

The TOR network runs on a distributed system. For the protection of your communications, data bounces around a relay of the distributed network that is made up of a lot of volunteers around the globe.

TOR runs from USB, and you can install it without having to download any software. It is also portable. You can surf the web anonymously, and even the website you visit will not be able to trace your physical connections.

zk-SNARKs

zk-SNARKs stands for Zero-Knowledge Succinct Non-Interactive Argument of Knowledge. The anonymity comes from the transaction validation process at play.

We have come across the blockchain technology working, and that validation involves some deanonymization. Well, all that changes with zk-SNARKs in that here, data can remain encrypted and still be verified successfully.

How does the validation occur?

Well, zk-SNARKs proofs allow the party with the burden of proof in a transaction to prove to the other person that they have a particular piece of information without revealing the data itself. For instance, if you have a specific digital key, you can prove that it is yours just by its validity and no additional information.

Transaction Mixing

The blockchain technology that Bitcoin runs in has a big anonymity problem that stems from the validation process. Transaction mixing is the solution to the problem.

The coin mixer can help by severing the connections between your previous and current addresses, hence making your transactions untraceable.

The anonymization process takes place when the mixer sends coins to other people and back to you. Coinmixer also increases delays in transactions and also makes transaction amounts randomly.

There are a few legitimate companies you can use. What you just need to do is send the Bitcoins to the company, plus their fee, and wait for them to send them back to you minus their output fee.

The input fee averages at 1% to 3%. The output fee is about 0.0016 BTC. The cost of anonymity is a bit high. The more coins you have, the more substantial the amount you fork over to cover expenses.

The only and the most dangerous downside to coin mixing is that you may end up with coins with a dark past. As we mentioned earlier, many crooked people are aiming to be anonymous, and you may end up with 'bad' coins.

Some of the legit Bitcoin mixers include Helix by grams, Bitcoin blender, Bitmixer.io, Bitcoin Fog and pay shield.

Recap: To this point, no system is completely anonymous. However, the above examples show that there is a lot of work going into making sure the anonymity dream comes to pass.

Chapter 6. Significant altcoins that use different anonymity as a selling point

There is no question that anonymity is a selling point for cryptocurrencies. As we have already seen, anonymity is attractive for a myriad of reasons, both good and bad.

It may have been a shock to you that Bitcoin is not as anonymous as you would have liked to imagine.

Some of these altcoins are presently doing very well due to the special anonymity features discussed in Chapter 6. Let us learn more about them.

Dash

This coin has undergone quite a bit of change before becoming the present day Dash. The name changed from Xcoin to Darkcoin before eventually becoming Dash.

Be careful not to confuse Dash and Dashcoin; they are not the same thing. Anonymity makes Dash attractive, and its value has been rising. There is speculation that in the long run, it may beat the crypto king, Bitcoin.

Some of the factors that affect the price of Dash include:

- The cryptocurrency market competition – as more and more coins join the market, the cost of Dash will fluctuate depending on the characteristics of other coins. If Dash can live up to its to the client's expectations, the price will increase. The reverse is also true.
- Increase in purchase – when Dash came into the market, there was a rush in its acquisition. The scramble to acquire the coin caused a price drop in line with the concept of demand and supply.
- Acceptance – the increased anonymity of Dash has made it much more acceptable than other cryptocurrencies. The crypto's price has been rising because the number of clients that prefer it keeps increasing.

  Below is a screenshot of the coin's performance. NB: A key to help you understand the screenshots.

  The market capitalization signifies the total value of the coin.

  The volume shows the value of trades in the coin in the last 24 hours.

  The circulating supply gives you the number of coins that are actively trading.

The maximum supply shows how many coins there are in total for the specific cryptocurrency.

This coin has had a wild ride last three months (October-December, 2017) as you can see below, but due to its technology, it is still going to do well in the future.

DASH/USD:

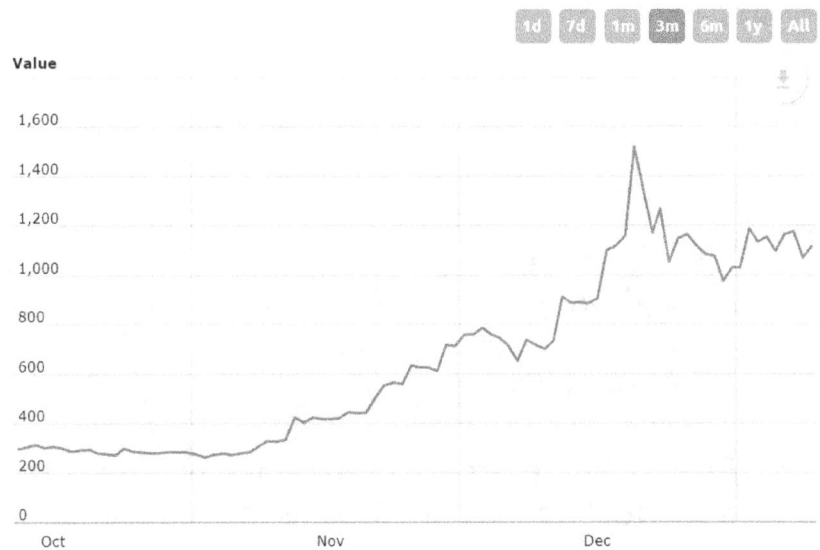

Source: worldcoinindex.com

ZCash (ZEC)

We have spoken a little bit about ZCash; it runs on zk-Snarks. The hype around Zcash's privacy feature raised the price of the coin even before its launch. This coin is a result of a Bitcoin fork.

The ZCash platform provides two types of addresses. There are private ones that shield the senders and recipients. They also have transparent addresses, which shows the balance in the recipients' accounts.

The shielded coins get to be more anonymous through a process known as fungibility. Fungible cryptocurrencies no longer have links to their blockchain history.

Buying Zcash with fiat currency is a bit difficult; you need to have other altcoins or Bitcoin to trade for Zcash.

At its launch, Zcash went for a whopping $2.3 million per coin. The price was a result of its highly publicised anonymity feature. The anticipation wore off, the coin's worth fell and is currently at $700.

ZEC/USD:

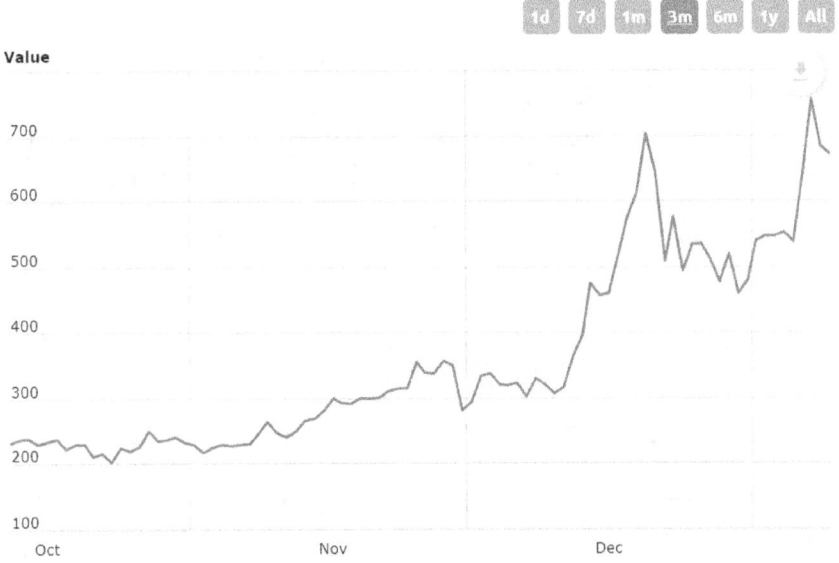

The most exciting aspect of the ICO was that the uptake of the shielded accounts was a lot less than expected. A vast majority of the early buyers opted for transparent addresses.

The coin still has a lot of potential due to its fungibility feature. With the increase in demand for anonymity, the coin's price is bound to increase.

Below are a few comparisons between Zcash and Bitcoin.

	Bitcoin (BTC)	Zcash (ZEC)
concept	Digital money	Private digital money
Transaction details	Publicity viewable	Concelated from public

Transaction example	Address X sent 1 btc to address Y	? sent ? zec to ?
Market cup (as of Dec 2017)	~$235 billion	~$900 ~million
Release date	Jan 2009	Oct 2016
Release method	mining	Mining w/ founders' reward

Source: Linda Xie on Medium

Monero (XMR)

 This coin is high up on the food chain, and it also has a bad rap for that. Sometime in mid-2017, there were cyber attacks that held companies' data ransom, and they would only accept Bitcoin as payment.

Due to all the criticisms of Bitcoins anonymity discussed above, the cybercriminals went a step further and converted the coins into Monero to make sure their identities would remain hidden.

Not only is Monero anonymous by design, it also offers the privacy of transactions. The recipient of a Monero doesn't even know who sent it to them. It is also not possible for someone to view your address and find out your transaction history or how much you own.

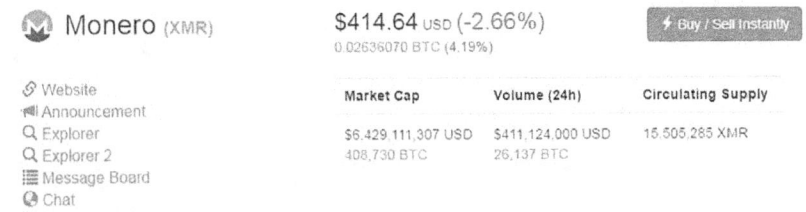

In summary, the distinguishing feature of this coin includes:

- It cannot be hacked,
- It has no block size limit,
- It is private, and most importantly,
- Untraceable

Monero has a few cards up its sleeve, such as its use in the darknet. Yes, you read that correctly. The deep, dark web is in the process of using the coin, and should the process be successful, the price could increase. The anonymity feature will be proven, and the coin will be more attractive.

The coin also intends to make use of I2P technology to increase anonymity. Additionally, bulletproofs are in development to help reduce transaction costs and an 80% increase in block size.

XMR/USD:

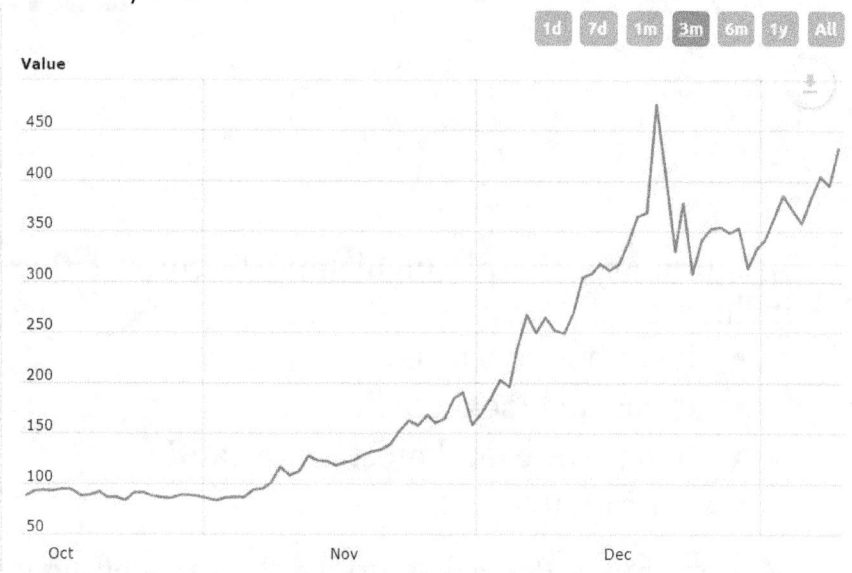

Source: worldcoinindex.com

Bytecoin (BCN)

Bytecoin works on the CryptoCoin technology.

Some of the factors that facilitate the growth of the altcoin include:

- Instant transactions – the coin claims to be as fast as the internet.
- Security of your money – the crypto algorithms in Bytecoin are unhackable, and therefore, you do not lose any of your hard-earned cash.
- Ability to process very large transactions – Bytecoin also promises that you will never have to worry about a limit on transaction amounts.

- Data security – anonymity protects your data, and with this altcoin, you should expect nothing less than total protection of your information. They claim nobody can see your information; you are the only one who can control it.

Bytecoin (BCN) $0.005637 usd (22.68%)   ⚡ Buy / Sell Instantly
0.00000036 BTC (31.43%)

§ Website
📢 Announcement
🔍 Explorer
🔍 Explorer 2
☰ Message Board
💬 Chat
🖥 Source Code

Market Cap	Volume (24h)	Circulating Supply	Max Supply
$1,033,036,825 USD	$21,338,500 USD	183,253,534,612	184,470,000,000
65,675 BTC	1,357 BTC	BCN	BCN

The coin seems to be having a good turn. It sure is going to have a bright 2018-01-04

BCN/USD:

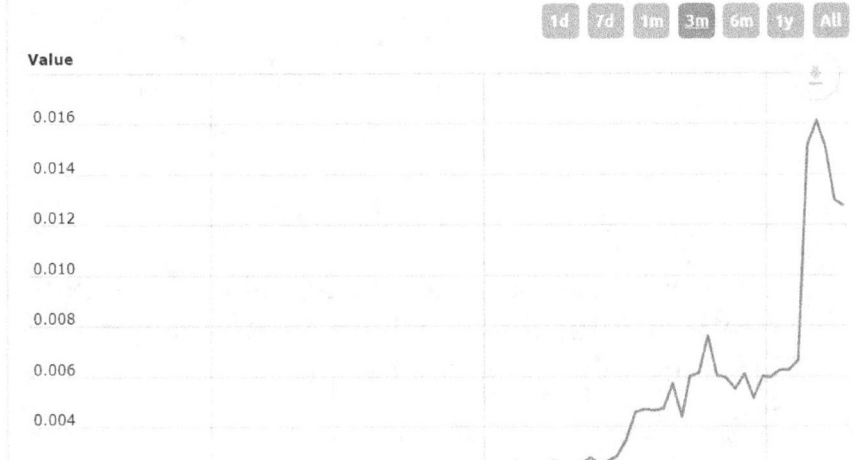

Source: worldcoinindex.com

Verge (XVG)

Transactions on Verge are fast, efficient and most importantly, private. Its anonymity comes from the coin's collaboration with sites like I2P and TOR, which are very big on anonymity.

The funds to run Verge do not come from pre-mined coins, but rather from a community of well-wishing enthusiasts from all over the world.

The coins price fluctuations are mostly as a result of the shift in the price of other major cryptos, like Bitcoin.

Verge (XVG)	$0.113549 USD (-9.91%) 0.00000722 BTC (-3.44%)	⚡ Buy / Sell Instantly

	Market Cap	Volume (24h)	Circulating Supply	Max Supply
	$1,640,603,716 USD 104,301 BTC	$515,607,000 USD 32,780 BTC	14,448,420,646 XVG	16,555,000,000 XVG

There was a lot of expectation about the launch of Wraith protocol on the 1st of January, 2018. Unfortunately, it was met with a price drop instead of an increase.

There is, however, a good chance the value of the coin will increase in the future. The wraith protocol is going to be beneficial to Verge users since it will allow them to choose when to be anonymous and when not to.

The feature may eventually bring the coin back up, as we can see below.

XVG/USD:

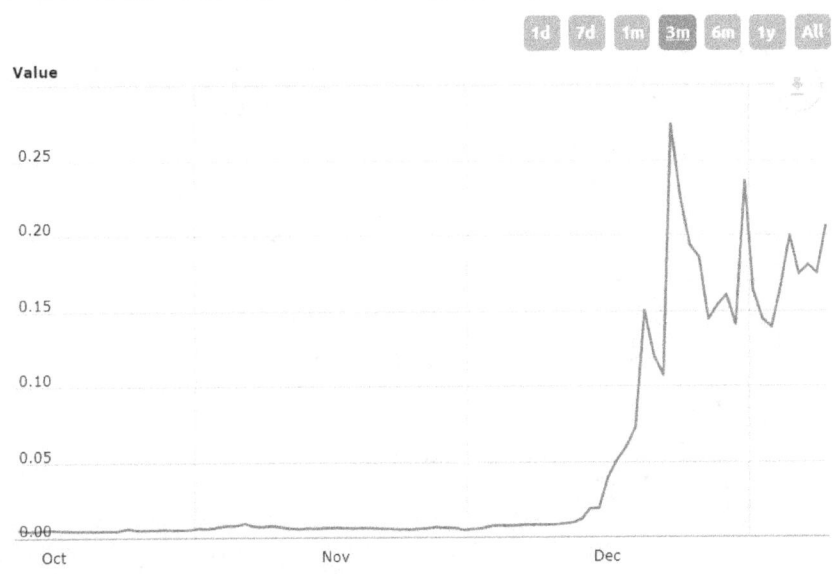

Source: worldcoinindex.com

PIVX

This coin's name comes from its promise of Private Instantly Verified transactions. PIVX hopes to provide better services than Bitcoin with regards to transaction times and client privacy.

PIVX came into being as a result of a Dash hard fork and is a better version of the former coin.

PIVX transactions are extremely fast compared to Bitcoin. They use Swiftx technology, which ensures almost instant transactions. The wait and confirmation time is also significantly reduced due to a network of master nodes.

PIVX works on the concept of proof of stake (PoS) as opposed to Bitcoin's proof of work. When using proof of work (PoW), the reward (payment) goes to the first mine to complete the mathematical problem. In proof of stake, however, there is no reward for blocks, only transaction fees.

Here we should compare main differences of PoS and PoW algorithms.

PoS vs PoW

The creation if a new coin in Bitcoin is called mining. Miners use expensive equipment to solve very complicated mathematical problems to complete a block. The first person to complete a block becomes that coin's miner. Miners in PoW networks get a transaction fee and a new block reward. To maximise their profit, miners select top-fee transactions from the transactions pool.

PoS, unlike PoW, eliminates the need for miners because transactions are validated by masternodes. Holders of large amount of coins could become a masternode and get a fee for transactions processing. Masternodes usually don't get any reward for a new block. All these changes eliminates a lot of PoW network disadvantages:

• Security. Anyone in a PoW network (even non-holders of coin) could process transactions and slow down network speed by generating and processing wrong transactions.

• High transaction fee. PoS network transactions are distributed between masternodes randomly. This eliminates the PoW issue where the transaction process time depends on the amount of fee and low-fee transactions that could be left unprocessed for days or even weeks

• Slow transactions. Mines are engaged in competition to resolve hard mathematical algorithms to get block rewards. It makes PoW networks energy inefficient because only first resolver is getting the reward. The rest of the miners receive nothing. PoS networks can be several thousand times more cost effective. The other side of this issue – PoW networks can process only 10-50 transactions/sec while PoS networks are much faster and can process more than 1000 transactions/sec (for example, Ripple network currently declares 1500+ transactions/sec).

PIVX (PIVX)

$9,10 USD (-23.34%)
0.00077256 BTC (-10.19%)

§ Website
📢 Announcement
🔍 Explorer
🔍 Explorer 2
🔍 Explorer 3
≡ Message Board
📖 Source Code
★ Rank 56
🏷 Coin

	Market Cap	Volume (24h)	Circulating Supply
	$503 584 244 USD	$12 828 500 USD	55,349,390 PIVX
	42,761 BTC	1,089 BTC	

PIVX/USD:

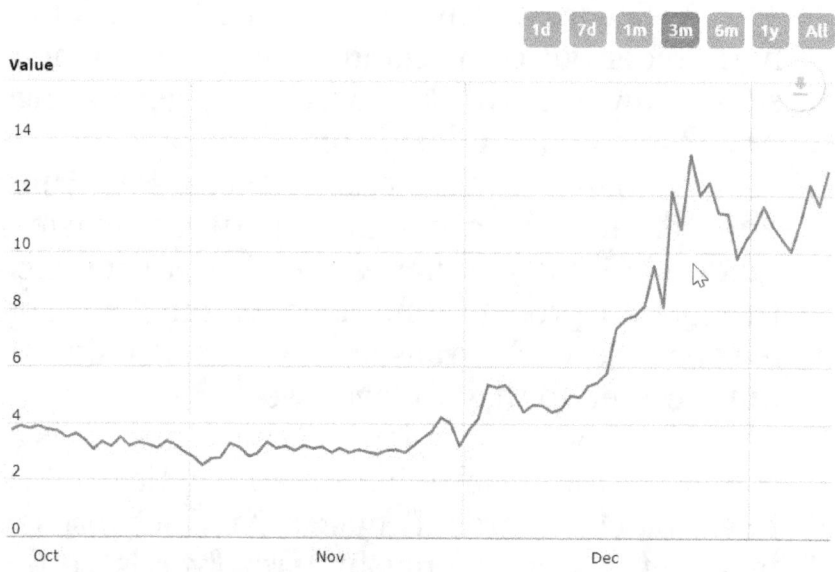

Source: worldcoinindex.com

Recap: There has been a gap in the cryptocurrency market. There are several selling points, such as decentralization, ability to perform huge transactions and just mere curiosity.

Recently, there has been a rise in the requirement for increased privacy and anonymity. The coins above have gone a step further than their predecessors, Bitcoin and Ethereum, in creating what clients need, and they are getting rewarded for their efforts by an increase in prices and market capitalization.

Conclusion

Transaction anonymity attracts more and more new users to the blockchain. Altcoin capitalization, which made anonymity one of their main advantages, has recently grown rapidly. One of the reasons for this increased interest in the cryptocurrency world is tightening control over the capital by the US and other governments. Therefore, many users prefer to transfer money from offshore to cryptocurrency. It is possible that in the future the crypto will even replace gold as a traditional way of preserving capital.

When buying and selling transactions take place, there are always people who want to keep their activity a secret. This is not always connected with something illegal, just the nature of humanity. So the demand for anonymous altcoins will grow, and their cost will rise. They are of interest, both for long-term investments and trading.

Blockchain has erased the border and has given all of us the opportunity to act directly, without intermediaries in the form of traditional financial institutions. But the world is changing, and it depends only on us whether we will change with it. The flexibility of thinking, the willingness to learn new things and adapt to change is something that everyone should bring to their life.

Use the resources provided here for more research. Read as many books and blogs as possible to understand what is happening in the world of cryptocurrencies.

The information is out there. The choice is yours!

Postface

Thank you for choosing my book among many others. I sincerely hope that you have found answers to your questions and learned a lot.

The cryptocurrency market is very volatile. It is working 24/7, and it requires constant analysis. I am going to publish a series of cryptocurrency books. The first book in the series appeared in the fall of 2017 and is dedicated to Bitcoin. I recommend reading it to everyone who wants to know more about blockchain revolution, cryptocurrency technologies, Bitcoin, and altcoins.

- In the first book of the series "Understanding Bitcoin" I explain the basic principles of how cryptocurrency works, talk about fraud schemes and share useful tips.
- What are the reasons for Bitcoin's growing value; its ups, and downs?
- What is behind it?
- What can we expect from Bitcoin in the future?
- How can we make money on cryptocurrencies?
- How can we avoid fraud schemes and scammers?

This book sorts out all the confusing information about cryptocurrency and makes it easier to understand. This is the minimum you should know before investing.

For getting in touch, information about updated editions, new books, or to send feedback, please follow me on social media:

Twitter: https://twitter.com/Scott_S_Bergman
Facebook: https://www.facebook.com/Scott-S-Bergman-1505759239510332/

And use this link or QR-kode
https://goo.gl/iPyuAE

If you enjoyed my book or benefited from it, I'd like to ask you for a favor. Please, take a few minutes to post an honest and heartfelt review on Amazon.com. I read all my reviews and would appreciate your thoughts.

Thank you in advance!

Sincerely yours,

Scott S. Bergman

**Investment opportunities come and go.
Now is the era of cryptocurrencies,
don't miss your chance!**